The Beach

by Frankie Hartley

We see the .

sun

We see the seal .

We see the .

bird

We see the .

wave

At the Beach

What can you see at the beach?
Tell a partner.

 ## Beach Picture

Draw a picture of the beach.
Label your picture.

Use Your Senses

Rebus • Lexile BR

Grade K • Unit 1 Week 3

www.mheonline.com

The **McGraw·Hill** Companies

ISBN-13 978-0-02-119374-5
MHID 0-02-119374-6

99701

EAN

9 780021 193745

K